MY FIRST

MUSIC
B·O·O·K

HELEN DREW

DK

DORLING KINDERSLEY
London • New York • Stuttgart

A Dorling Kindersley Book

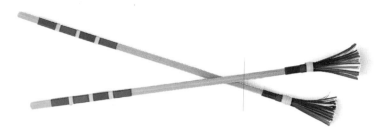

For my mother, Alison Broxholme

Designer *Mandy Earey*

Photography *Dave King*

Production *Jayne Wood*

Art Editor *Jane Coney*

Senior Editor *Nicola Tuxworth*

Managing Editor *Jane Yorke*

Managing Art Editor *Chris Scollen*

First published in Great Britain in 1993
by Dorling Kindersley Limited, London
9 Henrietta Street, London WC2E 8PS

**A CIP catalogue record for this book
is available from the British Library**

ISBN 0-7513-5027-3

Phototypeset by Setting Studio, Newcastle
Colour reproduction by Colourscan, Singapore
Printed and bound in Italy by L.E.G.O.

Dorling Kindersley would like to thank Alison Broxholme,
Lindsay Broxholme, Jonathan Buckley, Sharon Peters, Paul Gauntlett,
Peter Radcliffe, Vicky Watling, Jane Salt, Laura Cole, Jenny Cosgrave,
Oliver Cox, Cara Dack, Sam Drury, Daniel Fulcher, Daniel Geddes,
Anthea Hewitt-Springer, Billy Hunt, William Jones, Molly Kelly,
Sekunder Kermani, Alpa Kotecha, Shanna Nesbeth, Sebastian Ness,
Serina Palmer, Divya Pande, Laura Parry, Lucy Pearson,
Emma Redshaw, Dane Straw, Jessica Thorpe, Jessie Ware, Hannah Yate
and Alexia Zalaf for their help in producing this book.

Illustrations by Brian Delf

CONTENTS

MUSIC BY PICTURES   4

SIMPLE SHAKERS   6
SHAKERS, RATTLES AND
MARACAS   8

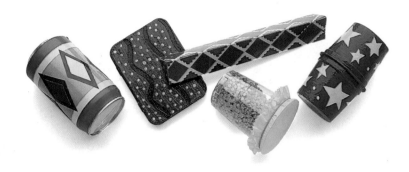

TINGLING TAMBOURINES   10
TAMBOURINE JAMBOREE   12

NOISY DRUMS   14
CRASH, BANG, WALLOP!   16

BEAT IT!   18

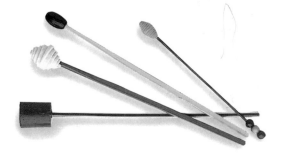

GUIROS ARE GREAT 20

MAKING A TRIANGLE 22

PENCIL XYLOPHONE 24

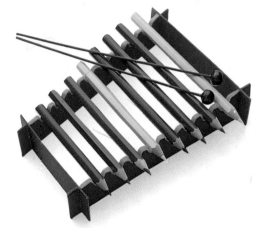

FLOWERPOT BELLS 26
A PEAL OF POTS 28

PIPE MUSIC 30

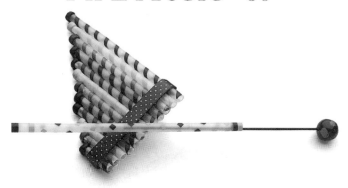

BUBBLE ORGAN 32

HORN PIPES 34
BLOW YOUR HORN 36

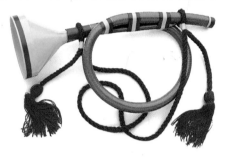

MUSICAL BOXES 38
STRING FEVER 40

MAKING A BANJO 42
BANJO MAGIC 44

MY FIRST ORCHESTRA 46

YOUNG COMPOSER 48

MUSIC BY PICTURES

My First Music Book is full of exciting musical instruments to make at home. Step-by-step photographs and simple instructions show you exactly what to do, and there are life-size photographs of all the things you need to collect and of the finished instruments. On the opposite page is a list of things to remember when using this book, and below you can find out what to look for in each project.

How to use this book

What the project is about
The introduction to each project tells you important information about the activity shown.

The things you need
The things to collect for each project are shown life-size to help you check that you have everything you need.

Step-by-step
Step-by-step photographs and clear instructions tell you exactly what to do at each stage of the project.

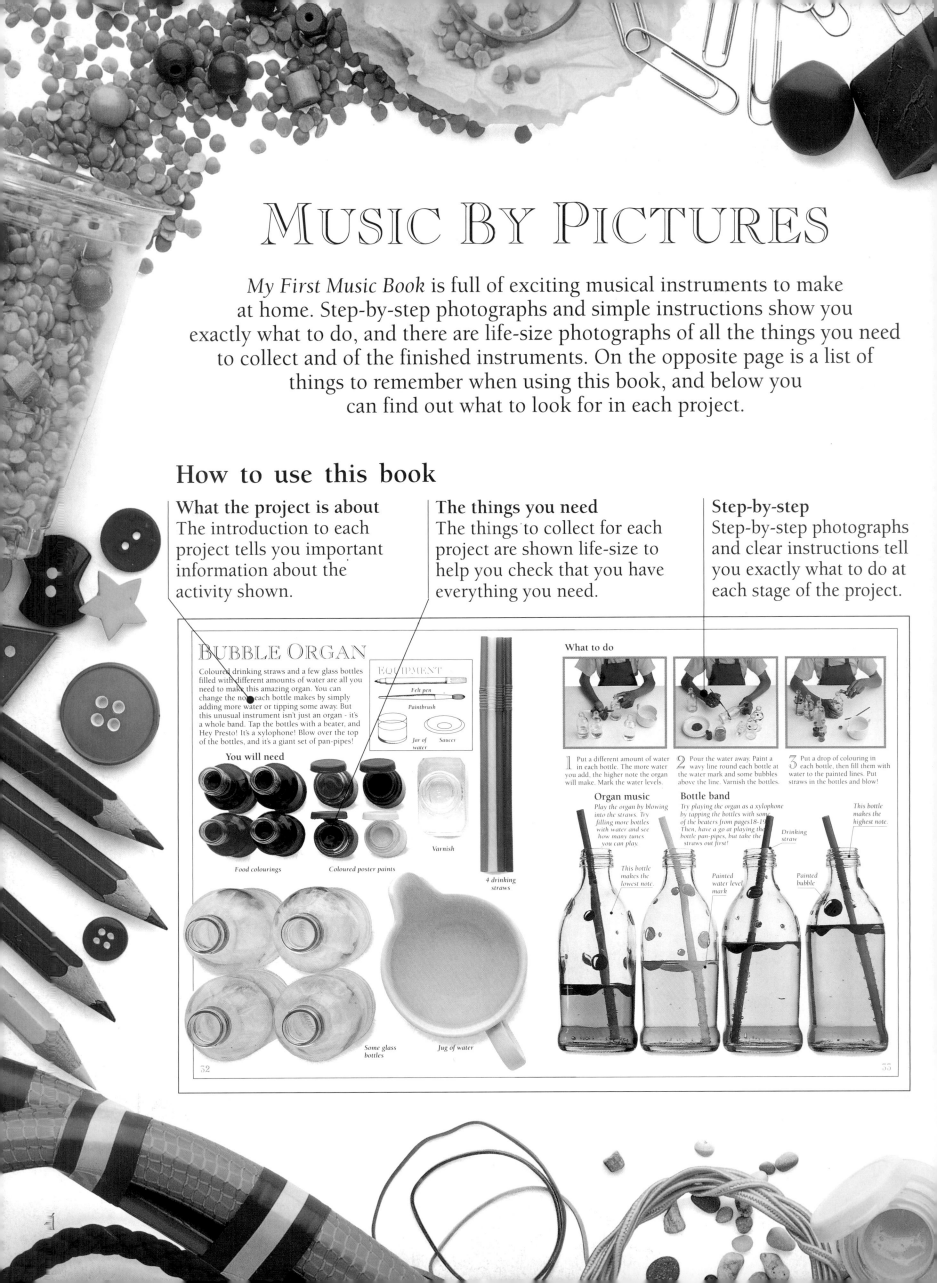

BUBBLE ORGAN

Coloured drinking straws and a few glass bottles filled with different amounts of water are all you need to make this amazing organ. You can change the note each bottle makes by simply adding more water or tipping some away. But this unusual instrument isn't just an organ - it's a whole band. Tap the bottles with a beater, and Hey Presto! It's a xylophone! Blow over the top of the bottles, and it's a giant set of pan-pipes!

EQUIPMENT

Felt pen

Paintbrush

Jar of water   Saucer

You will need

Varnish

Food colourings   *Coloured poster paints*

4 drinking straws

Some glass bottles   *Jug of water*

What to do

1 Put a different amount of water in each bottle. The more water you add, the higher note the organ will make. Mark the water levels.

2 Pour the water away. Paint a wavy line round each bottle at the water mark and some bubbles above the line. Varnish the bottles.

3 Put a drop of colouring in each bottle, then fill them with water to the painted lines. Put straws in the bottles and blow!

Organ music
Play the organ by blowing into the straws. Try filling more bottles with water and see how many tunes you can play.

Bottle band
Try playing the organ as a xylophone by tapping the bottles with some of the beaters from pages 18-19. Then, have a go at playing the bottle pan-pipes, but take the straws out first!

This bottle makes the lowest note.

This bottle makes the highest note.

Drinking straw

Painted water level mark

Painted bubble

Things to remember

1 Read the instructions before you start, to make sure you have everything you need.

2 Be very careful when using scissors and sharp knives. **Do not use them unless an adult is there to help you.**

3 Wash your hands and put on an apron or old shirt before you start, to protect your clothes.

4 Cover your work table with newspaper before you start to make anything.

5 When you have finished, wash up, put everything away, and clean up any mess.

6 Ask an adult to clean the varnish brush in white spirit for you.

7 Put the instruments away carefully when you have finished making them.

Equipment
Illustrated checklists show you which tools you will need to have ready before you start each project.

Playing steps
Look out for the special boxes. They show you how to play many of the instruments shown in this book.

The finished instrument
Life-size photographs show you what the finished instruments look like, making it easy for you to copy them.

PIPE MUSIC
Put a tune on your lips with these wonderful whistles. The note the whistle makes depends on how long its pipe is. The shorter the pipe, the higher the note it makes.

You will need

EQUIPMENT
Ruler
Paintbrush
Glue
Scissors
Jar of water
Saucer

Varnish

Coloured insulating tapes

1.5m plastic pipe

Red poster paint

Glue

White card

A wooden skewer

Coloured modelling clays

A large bead

Coloured ribbon

Whizz-it whistle

1 Cut a length of pipe about 25cm long. Decorate the pipe with thin strips and small diamonds of red and yellow tape.

2 Paint one skewer, then varnish it. Wind tape round one end of the skewer until it is wide enough to just fit inside the pipe.

3 Glue the bead onto the other end of the skewer. Rub a little petroleum jelly on the taped end, then push it into the tube.

Making pan-pipes

1 Cut off a 4cm piece of pipe, then cut 11 more pipes, each 1cm longer than the last. Wind tape in a spiral round each one.

2 Tape the pipes together, as shown. Glue a length of ribbon on to a strip of card, then glue the card on to the tape, to hide it.

3 Make 12 small balls of modelling clay. Push one ball firmly into the bottom of each pipe, so that no air can escape.

PAN-PIPING
Play the pan-pipes by blowing quickly to and fro along the pipes to make a quick series of notes, or try playing tunes by blowing over one pipe at a time.

Ribbon-covered strip of card

Coloured tape

Ball of modelling clay

Thin strip of tape

The petroleum jelly helps the slider move smoothly up and down inside the whistle.

Playing pipe whistles

Hold the pipes or whistle against your bottom lip, with your top lip pursed over it. Then blow a stream of air across the top of the pipe.

Small diamonds of coloured tape

WHOOSHING WHISTLE
Moving the slider in and out of the whistle as you blow over the top changes the note the whistle makes. Push the slider in to make a higher note and pull it out again to make a lower note.

Slider made from a wooden skewer and a bead

30

SIMPLE SHAKERS

You can make lots of different sounds with these simple instruments. All you have to do is fill a container with things that will rattle around inside it, and off you go! You can change the noise the shaker makes by changing the container or the filling you use. Here you can see all the fillings, containers and decorating ingredients we used. Look on the next page to see the finished shakers, rattles and maracas.

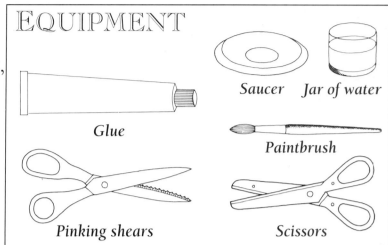
You will need

Containers:

Drinks can

Plastic container for gift ribbon

Small tin

2 yoghurt pots

Clear plastic beaker

Long cardboard box

Decorating ingredients:

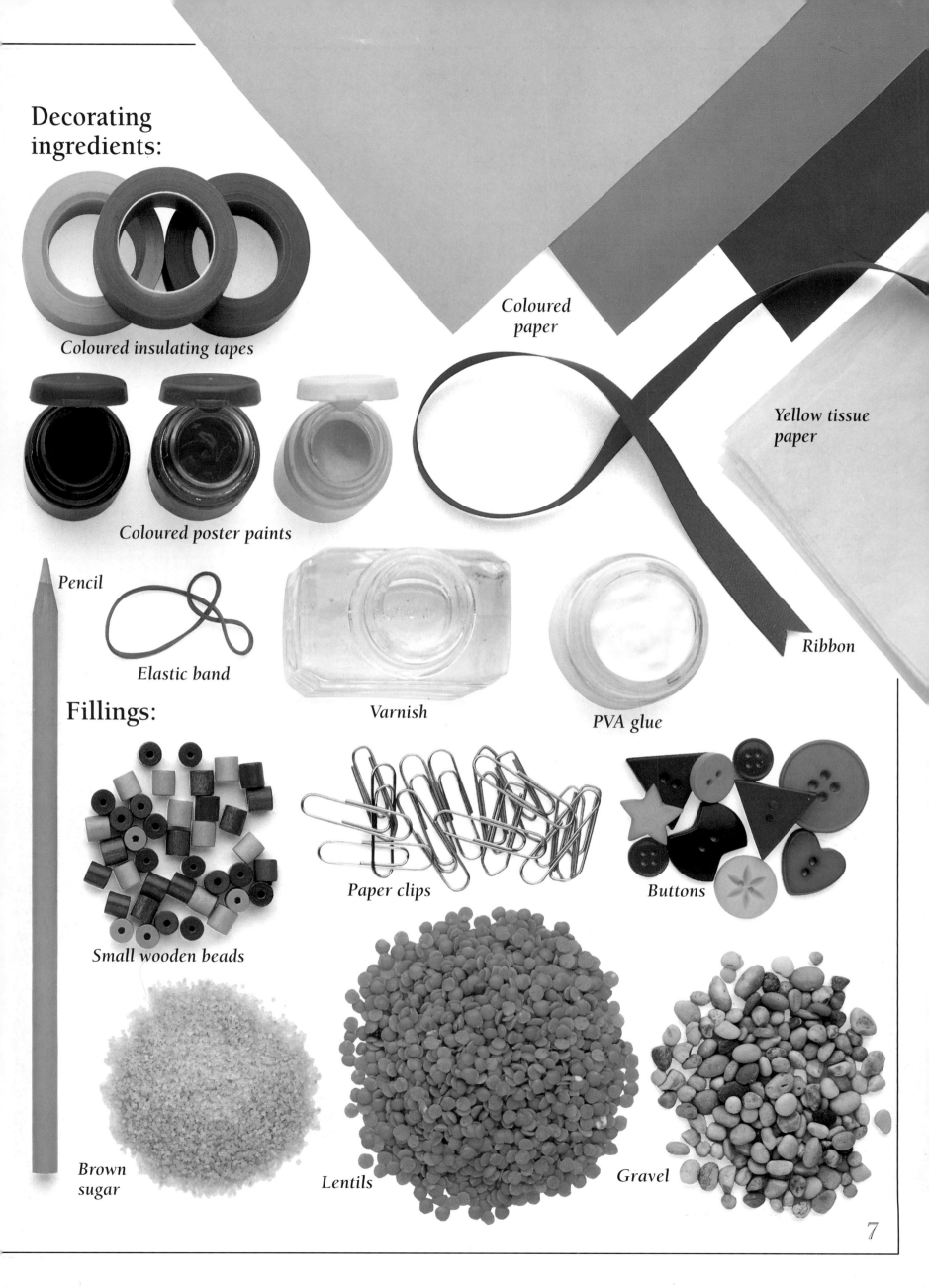

Coloured insulating tapes

Coloured poster paints

Coloured paper

Yellow tissue paper

Pencil

Elastic band

Varnish

PVA glue

Ribbon

Fillings:

Small wooden beads

Paper clips

Buttons

Brown sugar

Lentils

Gravel

SHAKERS, RATTLES AND MARACAS

Here are some ideas for making and decorating a whole range of shakers. If you read the labels, you will find out how to decorate each container and which filling to put inside. When you paint your plastic or metal containers, it is a good idea to mix the poster paints with some PVA glue, as this stops the paint flaking off later.

STAR SHAKER

This pretty shaker makes soft, swishing noises when you shake it. It is made by gluing two yoghurt pots together with a little sand or sugar inside. Paint the shaker with one colour at a time, letting each colour dry before using the next.

METAL MARACA

Metal containers and fillings make noisy shakers. This fizzy drinks can has a handful of paper clips inside. For a more unusual sound, try swirling the paper clips around inside the can.

Stick a circle of paper over the top of the can to cover the hole.

GRAVEL SLIDE

This long cardboard box is filled with gravel. Gently tip the box upside-down, and listen as the gravel slides around.

The squares of green tape were cut out using pinking shears.

Painted yellow stars

Small squares of blue tape

Strip of yellow tape

Strip of green paper

Big squares of yellow paper were glued on to the box.

Small, red paper diamond

Small, yellow paper diamond

Large, blue paper diamond

Slide the bottom half of the ribbon container on to the pencil. Wind tape thickly round the pencil on either side of the container, to hold it in place.

BEAD MARACA
This bead-filled shaker has a pencil handle.

Stick the two halves of the ribbon container together with tape.

A red elastic band holds the tissue paper circles tightly in place.

SUNSHINE SHAKER
This brightly coloured shaker makes a soft sound when you shake it.

The circles of yellow tissue were cut out with pinking shears to give them a zig-zagged edge.

Coloured wooden beads

Fluff out the edges of the tissue paper to make a frill.

Clear, plastic beaker with lentils inside.

Ribbon streamer

BUTTON BOX
This loud rattle is just a tin filled with plastic buttons. The tin was painted with poster paints mixed with PVA glue, then varnished once the paint was dry.

Yellow pencil has a thin strip of red tape wound around it.

Painted yellow spots

Tin painted red

Blue, painted wavy lines

9

TINKLING TAMBOURINES

For hundreds of years, dancers and singers have been shaking their brightly coloured tambourines in time to the music. Below, you can find out how to make two tambourines from papier-mâché. You will need to leave the tambourines to dry for three or four days before you can paint them. If you turn the page, you can see the finished instruments.

You will need

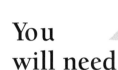

2 m of coloured ribbon

EQUIPMENT

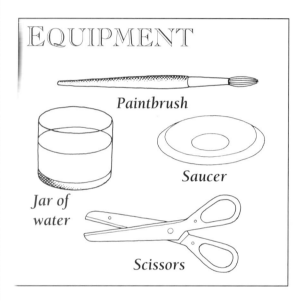

Paintbrush

Saucer

Jar of water

Scissors

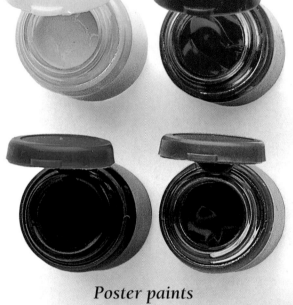

Poster paints

Varnish

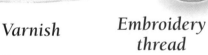

Embroidery thread

A wooden skewer

Bell tambourine

1 Spread petroleum jelly thickly over the outside of the baking ring. Tear sheets of newspaper into small, rectangular pieces.

2 Stick pieces of newspaper to the ring with paste. Make sure that the pieces overlap each other, so that there are no gaps left.

3 Build up layers of paper until the paper ring is 0.5 cm thick. Leave the ring to dry for two days, then slide it off the baking ring.

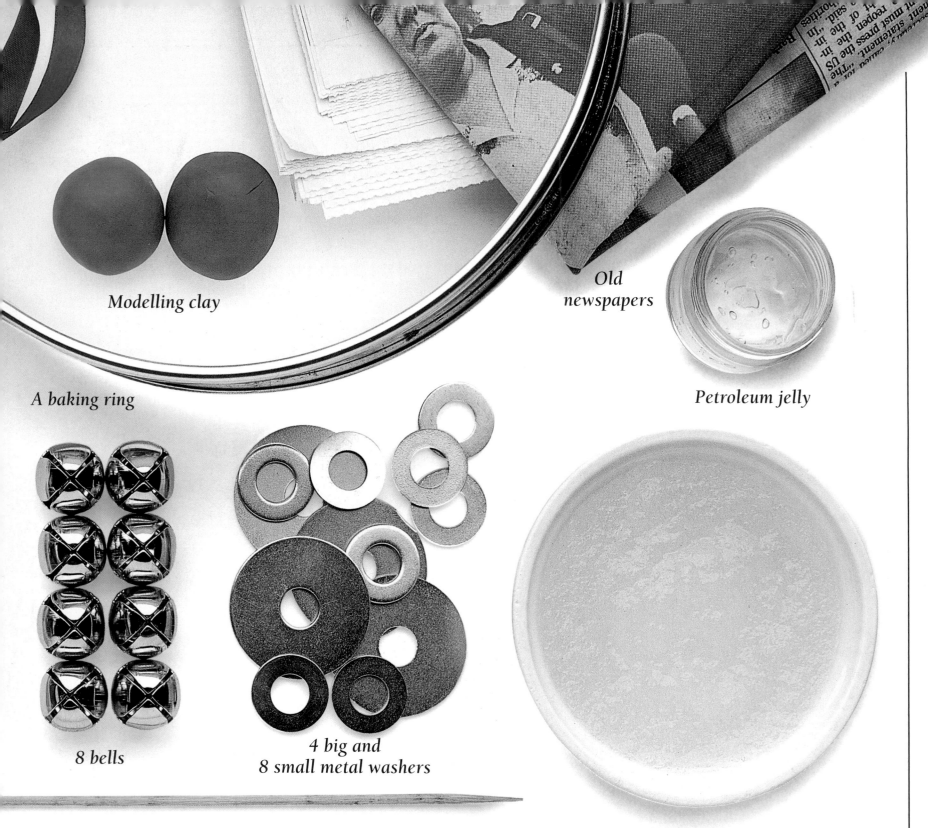

Modelling clay

Old newspapers

Petroleum jelly

A baking ring

8 bells

4 big and 8 small metal washers

Wallpaper paste*

Washer tambourine

1 Spread petroleum jelly over the ring. Press on four sausages of clay, as shown. Paste paper pieces to the ring, until it is 0.5cm thick.

2 When the paper is dry, peel off the sausages and slide the papier-mâché off the baking ring. Cut the wooden skewer in four.

3 Thread one big and two small washers on to each skewer piece and stick to each hole in the ring with layers of papier-mâché.

Ask an adult to mix the paste for you. Always wash your hands after using the paste.

TAMBOURINE JAMBOREE

Finishing off

Cut off the rough edges around the paper rings. Stick two layers of newspaper along the trimmed edges and leave the rings to dry.

Painting tambourines

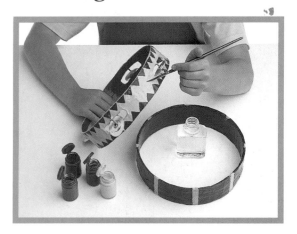

Paint the rings with poster paints. Do the outsides first and leave them to dry, then paint the insides. Varnish the rings in the same way.

Final touches

When the varnish is dry, tie bells on to the plain ring with coloured thread. Then tie on lengths of coloured ribbon.

And here are the finished tambourines! When the varnish has dried, the tambourines are ready to play. First, try shaking them in the air. Then hold the tambourine in one hand and tap it against the palm of your other hand, in time to some music. You can see children playing both tambourines in our orchestra on pages 46 and 47.

Washer tambourine

As you shake this tambourine, the washers rattle against each other and make a lovely jingling sound.

Washer jingles

SWALLOW TAILS

Cutting a 'V'-shape into the ends of the ribbons stops the ribbons fraying and looks very pretty, too!

VARNISHING ACT

Varnishing the tambourine makes it much stronger, and protects the painted decorations against damage.

12

RIBBON STREAMERS
Knot two long pieces of coloured ribbon around each bell.

BELL ROPE
Tie the bells on to the ring with thread the same colour as the paint you have chosen.

Silver bell

Jingle bells
The bells make a bright, light, tinkling sound when you shake the tambourine. Try tying bells of two different sizes to the ring for a two-tone sound.

13

Noisy Drums

Jump to the beat with two loud and colourful drums to make! Below, you can see everything you need for making a really professional tin drum and a fantastic flowerpot tom-tom. Turn the page to see the finished drums, and to find out how to make a drum-kit.

Equipment

Pencil

Scissors

You will need

2 plastic flowerpots

Making the tin drum

1 Decorate the side of the tin with coloured paper and thin strips of tape. Stick the red cord to opposite sides of the tin with tape.

2 Cut off the end of a balloon. Ask an adult to help you stretch the balloon over the open tin. Then quickly tape it to the tin sides.

Making the tom-tom

1 Draw round a pot on muslin, then draw a circle 2cm bigger around it. Draw a third circle 2 cm bigger around the second circle.*

* Repeat this step on a second piece of muslin.

A round
cake or biscuit tin

Coloured
paper

White cotton
muslin

Red dressing-gown cord

5m thin
gold cord

Yellow
insulating tape

Giant blue balloon

Rubber solution glue

2 Cut out the circles around the outer line. Cover the pots with coloured paper, then stick them together with tape, as shown.

3 Make lots of small cuts round the edge of both circles, in to the 2cm line. Spread glue from the edge to the flowerpot circle.

4 Fold in the cut edges of each circle, as shown, to make a hem. Make 16 evenly spaced holes with a pencil round the hem.

CRASH, BANG, WALLOP!

What to do

The tin drum and tom-tom are ready to play. To begin with, just tap the drums with your fingertips. Then, turn the page to find out how to make lots of different drumsticks and beaters that will make the drums sound even better. Experiment by hitting each drum with a different drumstick.

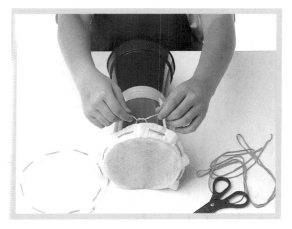

5 Thread cord through the holes in each circle. Put a circle on one pot, pull the cord tight and tie a knot. Repeat with the other pot.

Don't hit the drum skin too hard, or the balloon may burst.

Smart, red drum cord

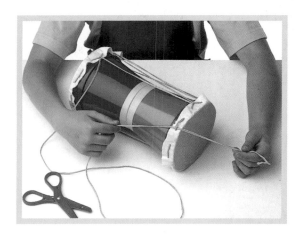

6 Thread a long piece of cord through a loop on one circle to a loop on the other and back up again, as shown, around the drum.

Yellow tape holds the balloon skin in place.

7 Pull the cord tight all round the drum, then knot it. Spread glue over the cloth, then tighten the cord again. Leave glue to dry*.

A strip of green, shiny paper covers the tin.

Thin strip of yellow tape

Square of red paper

PLAYING THE TIN DRUM

If you put the drum cord over your head, you can play your drum as you walk around.

*Hang the drum up to dry by its cord, so that the drum won't stick to anything.

Shiny, green paper hides the plastic flowerpot underneath.

A drum kit

Try making lots of drums with tins of different sizes, then put them together to make a drum kit. Each drum makes a different sound.

PLAYING THE TOM-TOM

Hold the tom-tom under your arm or between your knees, then tap one end of the drum with the flat of your fingers. You can see someone playing this tom-tom on page 47.

Yellow insulating tape sticks the two flowerpots together.

The gold cord pulls the drum skins tight.

Blue tape

Red, shiny paper

When the glue dries, it forms an airtight skin on the muslin. This makes the tom-tom sound louder.

17

BEAT IT!

On this page you can see all the beaters you will need to play the instruments in this book. They are all very quick and easy to make. Read the labels to find out what to do, or try out some ideas of your own. Experiment by playing your instruments with both hard and soft beaters, and listen to the different sounds they make.

DOUBLE BEATER

These beaters have a soft, felt end and a hard, wooden bead end.

Painted and varnished wooden skewer

A tall triangle of felt rolled round and round a wooden skewer, then glued down.

Red, yellow and blue wooden beads are glued on to a wooden skewer.

Yellow sponge cloth

SOFT SPONGE BEATERS

Cut out a tall triangle of sponge cloth 3cm wide and 15cm long. Roll it round and round one end of a chopstick, then glue it down.

Chopstick painted blue, and then varnished.

CORK BEATERS

These simple beaters are just chopsticks with a large cork glued on one end.

The cork was painted red, and then varnished.

Cut lots of slits into short lengths of drinking straw, then tape them round one end of a chopstick.

Thin strip of green insulating tape

Thin strip of red insulating tape

Thin strips of red, yellow and blue insulating tape

18

STRAW BRUSHES

Try using these brushes on the tom-tom on page 17.

Decorate a wooden chopstick with strips of coloured insulating tape.

Painted and varnished wooden skewer

BIG DRUM BEATER

The ball of the drumstick is made from a circle of felt, filled with cotton wool.

Wooden bead glued on to the pointed end of the skewer.

Four small, metal nuts glued on to a chopstick.

XYLOPHONE BEATERS

You can find out how to make the pencil xylophone on pages 24-25.

Wind an elastic band tightly round the felt to make a ball, then push the knitting needle inside.

Yellow thread hides the elastic band.

NUT BEATERS

These hard beaters work best on the bottle xylophone. Don't hit the bottles too hard, or they will break.

This blue, oval bead has a wide hole through its middle.

DRUMSTICKS

These beaters are just chopsticks with a bead glued on one end. Try them on the tin drum on page 16.

This chopstick was painted red, and then varnished.

The handle is a big knitting needle, painted red, then decorated with a strip of yellow tape.

Chopstick painted yellow, and then varnished.

19

GUIROS ARE GREAT!

These colourful, South American instruments are great fun to play. Guiros (pronounced gweer-ohs) have special, ridged surfaces that make a wonderful, rasping noise when you scrape them. Here you can find out how to make two different guiros and their scrapers.

You will need

Glue

Lots of small beads*

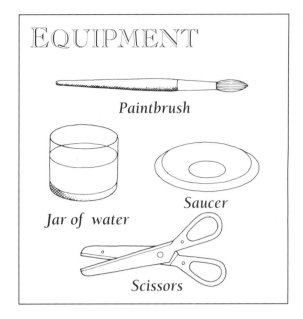

Paintbrush

Jar of water

Saucer

Scissors

Plant label

A cork

A large, blue bead

Poster paints

1m of coloured ribbons

1m of cord

2 wooden skewers

Small plastic bottle

Varnish

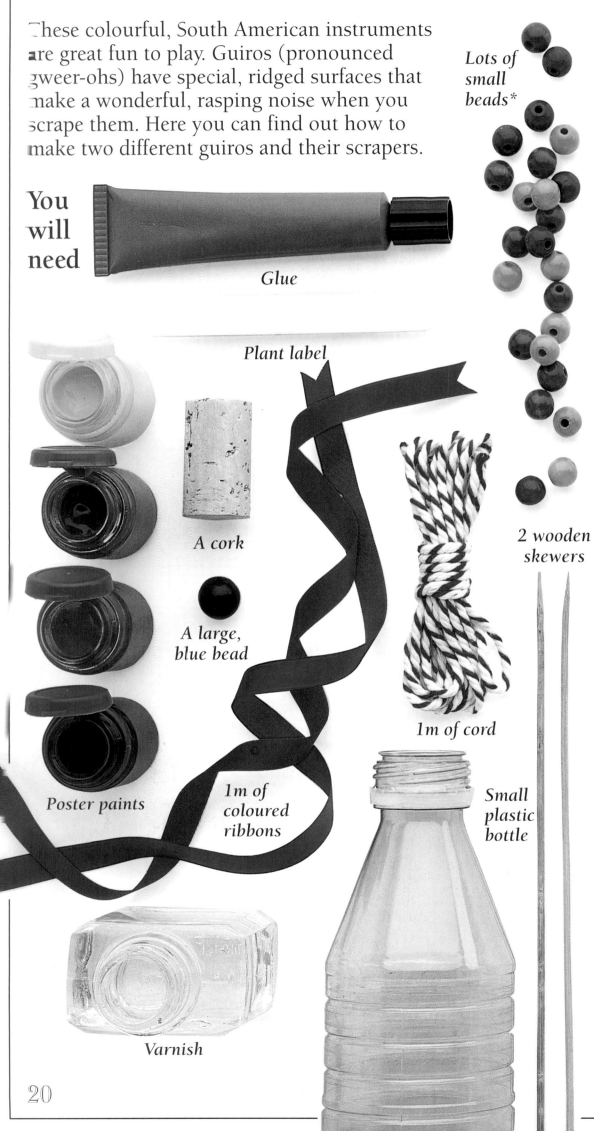

Bottle guiro

1 Paint a design on the bottle and leave it to dry. Wind cord round the bottle and glue it in place, then varnish the bottle.

2 To make the bottle scraper, paint a plant label, then varnish it. Wind cord round one end and glue the loose ends down.

*Make sure the holes in the beads are wide enough to fit on the wooden skewer.

Bead guiro

1 Stick the pointed end of one skewer deep into the cork. Paint the cork and then varnish it, once the paint is dry.

2 Thread beads on to the skewer. Put the big bead on last and glue it in place. Tie some ribbons between the cork and the first bead.

3 To make the bead scraper, paint another skewer and varnish it. When the varnish is dry, glue a bead on to the pointed end of the skewer.

BEAD GUIRO

This guiro is made of wooden beads. You can change the sound the guiro makes by varying the shapes and sizes of the beads, or by using plastic or metal ones instead.

Experiment with rhythms by scraping the guiro backwards and forwards, first quickly and then slowly, using long and short strokes of the scraper.

Cut a 'V'-shape into the ends of ribbons to stop them fraying.

BOTTLE GUIRO

To play this instrument, hold the bottle in the palm of your hand and drag the plastic scraper along the surface. The bottle's hollow inside acts like a loudspeaker. If you put the top back on the bottle and play the guiro, it sounds much quieter.

Large, blue bead

Bead handle

Plant label scraper

Varnishing the bottle stops the paint flaking off.

Hold the guiro by its cork handle.

Colourful ribbons are knotted round the skewer.

MAKING A TRIANGLE

This simple triangle and its striker are made from coach bolts, which you can buy at any hardware shop. The triangle makes a bright chiming sound when you hit it with the striker.

You will need

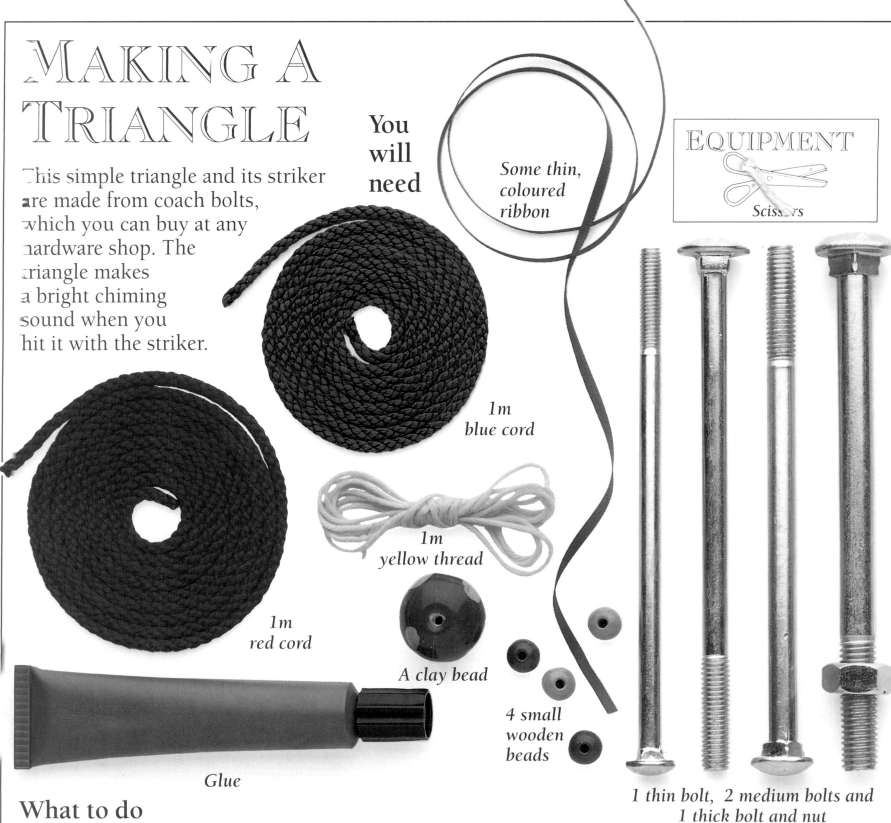

Some thin, coloured ribbon

1m blue cord

1m yellow thread

1m red cord

A clay bead

4 small wooden beads

Glue

1 thin bolt, 2 medium bolts and 1 thick bolt and nut

What to do

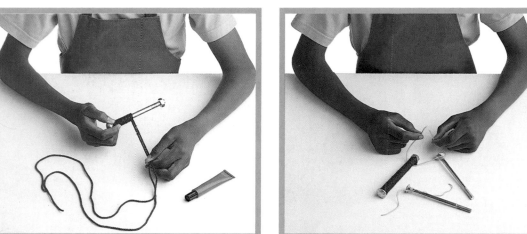
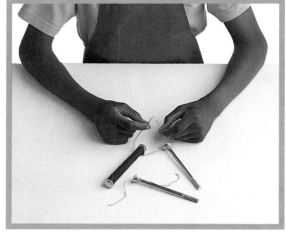

1 For the handle, wind red and blue cord together on to the thick bolt and nut, as shown. Glue the ends of the cords to the bolt.

2 Wind thread round the top of each medium bolt, and knot it tightly. Tie a bolt to each end of the handle, leaving each to hang freely.

3 Wind a piece of thread in the grooves of the bolt, as shown. Knot the thread tightly at the bottom and glue it to the bolt.

Making the striker

 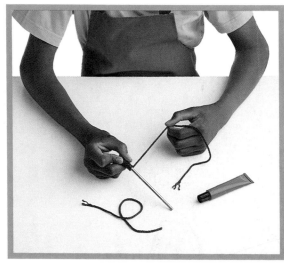 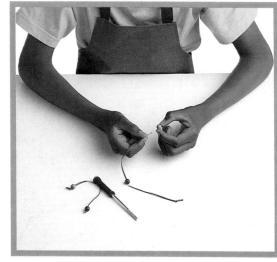

4 Thread on the clay bead and tie the free end of the thread to the other medium bolt. Glue the thread into the grooves of the bolt.

1 Spread glue around the top half of the thin bolt, then wind red cord on top. Glue one turn of blue cord at the end. Leave to dry.

2 Thread two beads on to two ribbons. Tie knots in the ends. Tie the ribbons securely to the top end of the striker.

Playing the triangle

You play the triangle by hitting it with the striker. Make a ringing noise by moving the striker quickly back and forth between the bolts.

Push one bead to each end of the ribbons.

Striker handle

Tuneful Triangles

You can make a two-note triangle by using a thin and a medium bolt, instead of the two medium bolts used here.

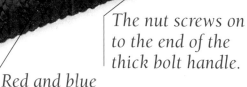

The nut screws on to the end of the thick bolt handle.

Red and blue cord handle

The bolts must hang free on the threads, without touching the handle of the triangle.

Thread is glued in the grooves of the bolts to stop the knots coming undone.

For a softer sound, try hitting the triangle with the handle of the striker.

The heavy, clay bead pulls the bolts together to make a triangular shape.

PENCIL XYLOPHONE

Here you can find out how to make a mini-xylophone with a few coloured pencils. You tune the xylophone by sharpening the pencils to different lengths. The shorter you make the pencil, the higher the note it will make when you hit it with a beater.

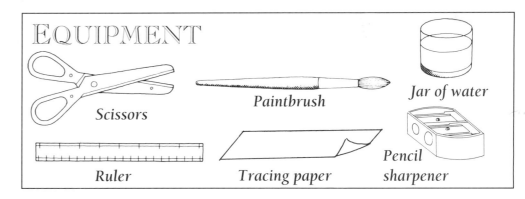
Template for the two sides of the frame

Template for the long end of the frame

Template for the short end of the frame

You will need

Red poster paint

Rubber solution glue

Thick, coloured card

Yellow felt

Eight coloured pencils (Thick pencils make the best noise.)

What to do

1 Trace the templates for the four pieces of the frame on to thick card, then cut them out. Paint one side of the card.

2 Slot the frame together, as shown. Cut two strips of felt 0.5 cm wide and 30 cm long. Glue the felt along the top of the frame.

3 Sharpen the pencils so that each one is about 0.5 cm shorter than the one before it. Put the pencils in order, on the frame.

Pencils on parade

Play the xylophone by dragging the beater to and fro along the pencils to play a scale. You can play a tune by striking the pencils, one at a time, with a beater.

XYLOPHONE BEATERS
The beaters are wooden skewers with a wooden bead glued on one end. The handles were painted red, and then varnished.

The inside of the frame is painted red.

Strip of yellow felt

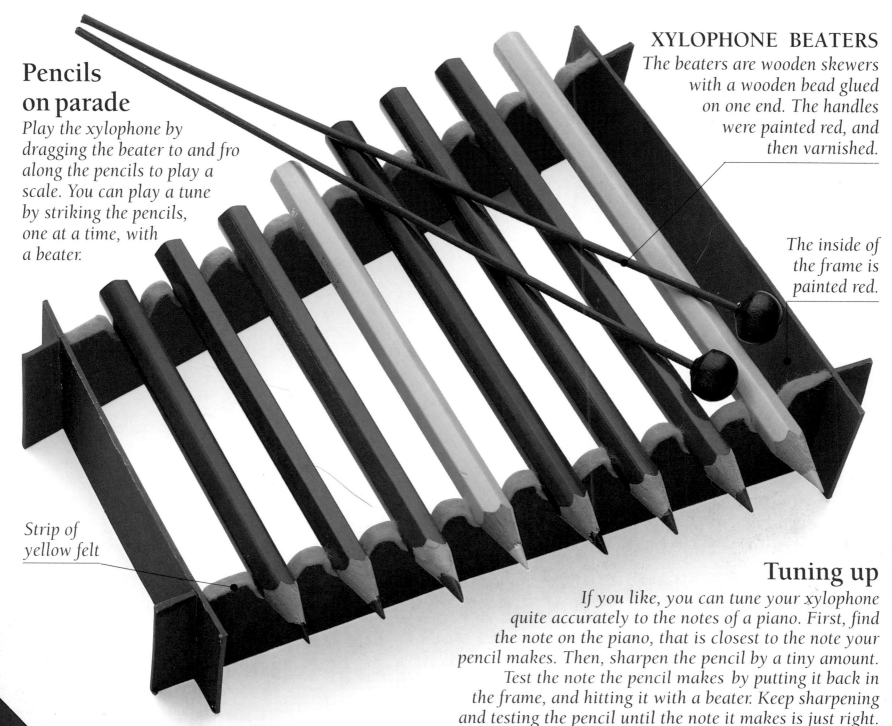

Tuning up
If you like, you can tune your xylophone quite accurately to the notes of a piano. First, find the note on the piano, that is closest to the note your pencil makes. Then, sharpen the pencil by a tiny amount. Test the note the pencil makes by putting it back in the frame, and hitting it with a beater. Keep sharpening and testing the pencil until the note it makes is just right.

25

FLOWERPOT BELLS

Terracotta flowerpots make a wonderful ringing noise when they are hit with a beater, and every pot produces a different note. Below you can see everything you will need to turn a few flowerpots into a hand bell and a set of tuneful hanging bells.

Start by collecting a few terracotta pots. If you don't have any pots at home, you can buy them very cheaply at your local garden centre. Choose flowerpots of different sizes. The small pots make high notes when they are rung and the big ones make low notes. Turn the page to see all the bells and find out how to ring them.

You will need

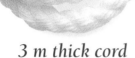

3 m thick cord

A pencil

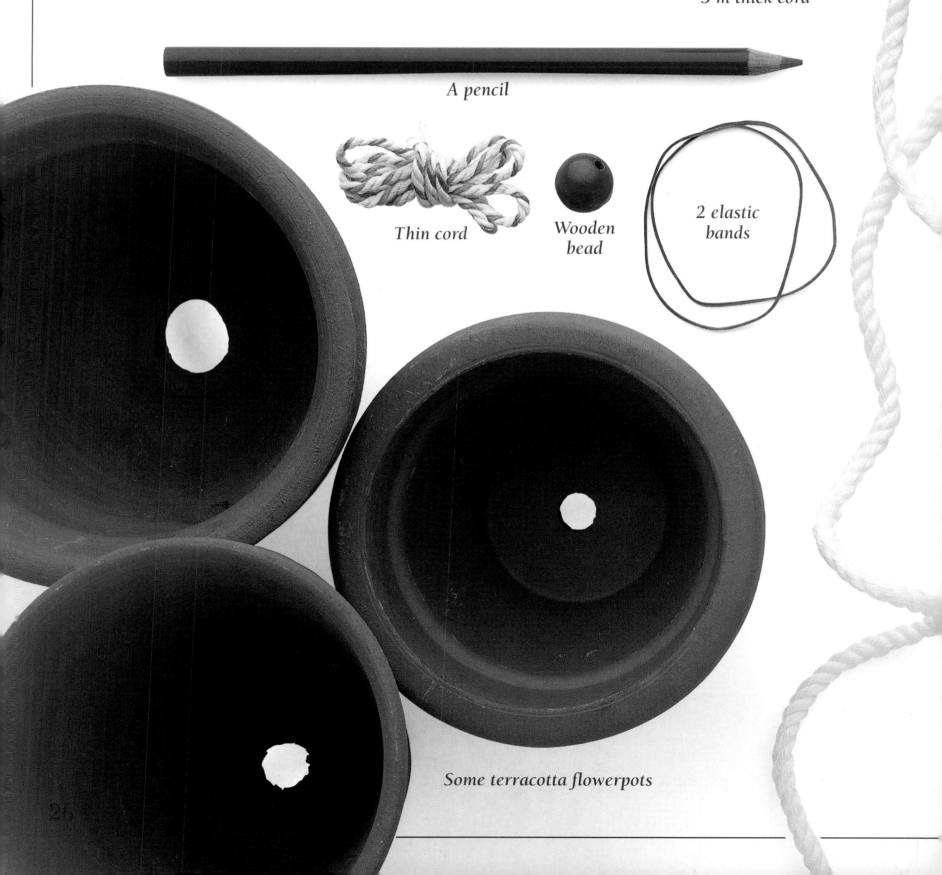

Thin cord

Wooden bead

2 elastic bands

Some terracotta flowerpots

Coloured poster paints

Coloured insulating tape

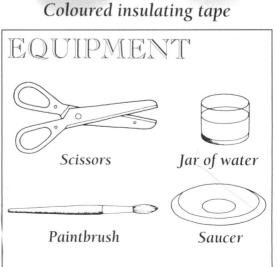
Hanging bell

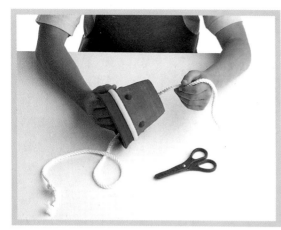

1 Paint colourful patterns on the flowerpots and leave them to dry. Cut a piece of thick cord, about 75cm long, for each pot.

2 Tie a knot in one end of each cord. Thread the cord through the hole in the bottom of each pot, as shown.

Handbell

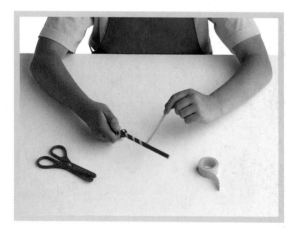

1 Thread a bead on to a piece of thin cord and tie a knot in one end. Tape the cord to the pointed end of the pencil.

2 Keep winding tape round the pencil until it is wider than the small hole in the pot. Decorate the pencil with a spiral of tape.

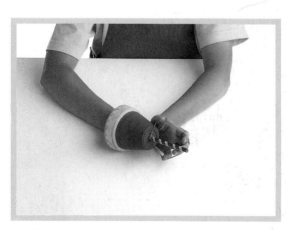

3 Paint a design on the flowerpot. Let each colour dry before painting on another. Push the pencil through the hole in the pot.

4 Wind the elastic bands round and round the pencil, then push them down so that they sit tightly against the flowerpot.

27

A Peal Of Pots

When you have finished your flowerpot bells, it's time to hang them up. Rest an old broom handle across two chairs, then tie the bells to it by their cords. In the playing step, you can see another way to hang the bells - by knotting two pots on to a single length of cord and holding the cord yourself. You will need beaters to play the hanging bells, so look on pages 18 and 19 for lots of ideas.

This pot is bell-shaped!

Handbell
Try making several handbells of different sizes, then see if you can play a tune with them.

Playing hanging bells

First, try striking the outside of the bell with a beater. Then, put the beater inside the bell and move it quickly backwards and forwards.

Elastic bands pushed tightly up against the flowerpot.

RING THAT BELL
Hold the handbell by its pencil handle and shake the bell, so that the bead hits the inside of the flowerpot.

Tiny triangles painted around the rim

Yellow insulating tape

Red pencil

LOOK, NO PAINT!
Flowerpot bells look good unpainted, too.

Paint the handbell with colourful patterns

Twin bells

To make twin bells, tie a big knot further up the cord of one bell, then thread on a second pot.

Thick, white cotton cord

Hanging bells

Tie the bells to the broom handle so that they all hang at different heights. This will make the bells easier to play.

KNOTS NEEDED

The bells are quite heavy, so make sure that you tie good, strong knots when attaching your bells to the broom handle.

PIPE MUSIC

Put a tune on your lips with these wonderful whistles. The note the whistle makes depends on how long its pipe is. The shorter the pipe, the higher the note it makes.

EQUIPMENT

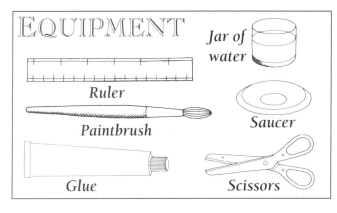

Ruler

Paintbrush

Glue

Jar of water

Saucer

Scissors

You will need

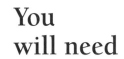

Varnish

Coloured modelling clays

Red poster paint

Petroleum jelly

White card

A wooden skewer

A large bead

Coloured ribbon

Coloured insulating tapes

1.5m plastic pipe

Whizz-it whistle

1 Cut a length of pipe about 25cm long. Decorate the pipe with thin strips and small diamonds of red and yellow tape.

2 Paint one skewer, then varnish it. Wind tape round one end of the skewer until it is wide enough to just fit inside the pipe.

3 Glue the bead onto the other end of the skewer. Rub a little petroleum jelly on the taped end, then push it into the tube.

Making pan-pipes

1 Cut off a 4cm piece of pipe, then cut 11 more pipes, each 1cm longer than the last. Wind tape in a spiral round each one.

2 Tape the pipes together, as shown. Glue a length of ribbon on to a strip of card, then glue the card on to the tape, to hide it.

3 Make 12 small balls of modelling clay. Push one ball firmly into the bottom of each pipe, so that no air can escape.

PAN-PIPING

Play the pan-pipes by blowing quickly to and fro along the pipes to make a quick series of notes, or try playing tunes by blowing over one pipe at a time.

Ribbon-covered strip of card

Thin strip of tape

The petroleum jelly helps the slider move smoothly up and down inside the whistle.

Coloured tape

Ball of modelling clay

Playing pipe whistles

Small diamonds of coloured tape

WHOOSHING WHISTLE

Moving the slider in and out of the whistle as you blow over the top changes the note the whistle makes. Push the slider in to make a higher note and pull it out again to make a lower note.

Hold the pipes or whistle against your bottom lip, with your top lip pursed over it. Then blow a stream of air across the top of the pipe.

Slider made from a wooden skewer and a bead

BUBBLE ORGAN

Coloured drinking straws and a few glass bottles filled with different amounts of water are all you need to make this amazing organ. You can change the note each bottle makes by simply adding more water or tipping some away. But this unusual instrument isn't just an organ - it's a whole band. Tap the bottles with a beater, and Hey Presto! It's a xylophone! Blow over the top of the bottles, and it's a giant set of pan-pipes!

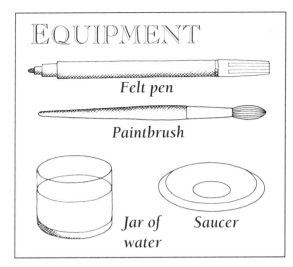

EQUIPMENT

Felt pen

Paintbrush

Jar of water   *Saucer*

You will need

Food colourings

Coloured poster paints

Varnish

4 drinking straws

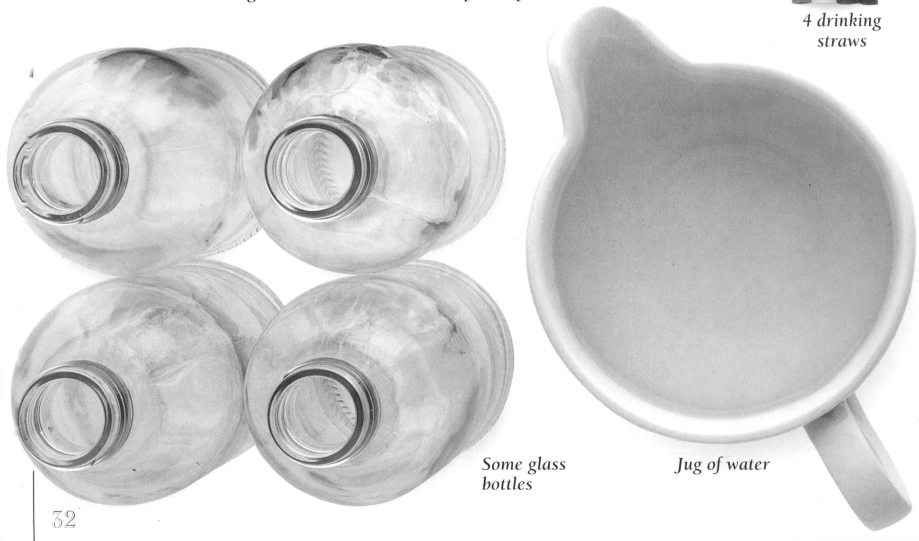

Some glass bottles

Jug of water

What to do

1 Put a different amount of water in each bottle. The more water you add, the higher note the organ will make. Mark the water levels.

2 Pour the water away. Paint a wavy line round each bottle at the water mark and some bubbles above the line. Varnish the bottles.

3 Put a drop of colouring in each bottle, then fill them with water to the painted lines. Put straws in the bottles and blow!

Organ music

Play the organ by blowing into the straws. Try filling more bottles with water and see how many tunes you can play.

Bottle band

Try playing the organ as a xylophone by tapping the bottles with some of the beaters from pages 18-19. Then, have a go at playing the bottle pan-pipes, but take the straws out first!

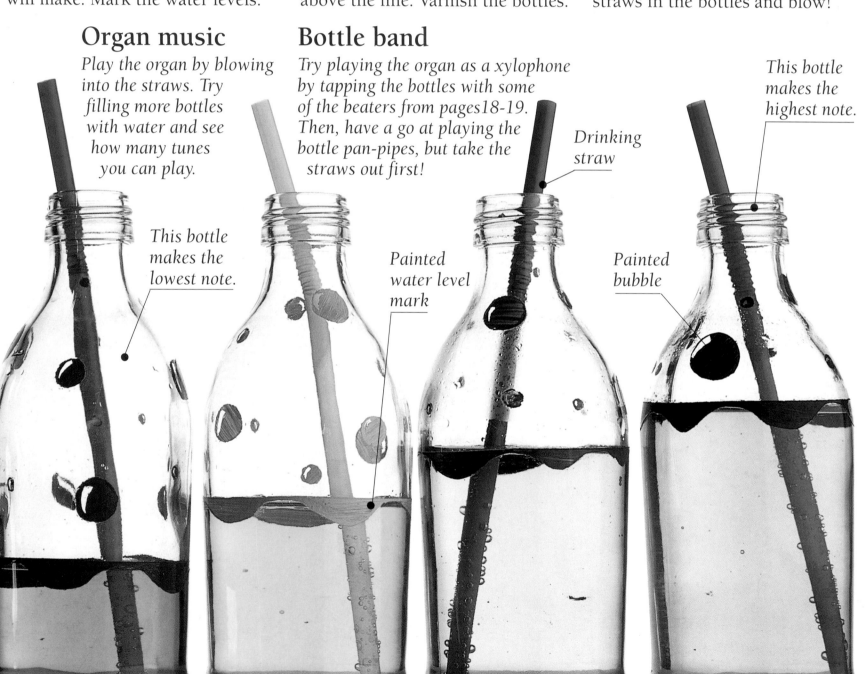

This bottle makes the highest note.

Drinking straw

This bottle makes the lowest note.

Painted water level mark

Painted bubble

33

Horn Pipes

Wind instruments such as horns, trumpets, didgeridoos and tubas are all made from long tubes. They are called wind instruments because you blow into them when you play them. Here, you can find out how to make a didgeridoo out of cardboard tubes and a horn from garden hose. On the next page you can see the finished instruments and find out how to play them.

You will need

A red dressing-gown cord

Two long cardboard tubes, about 4cm in diameter

Making the didgeridoo

EQUIPMENT

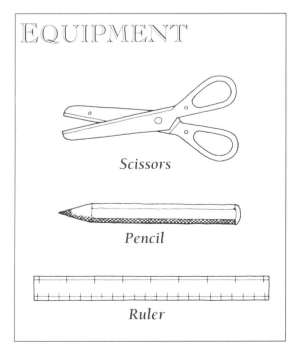

Scissors

Pencil

Ruler

1 Stick the ends of two cardboard tubes tightly together with tape, to make one long tube. Cover this tube with coloured paper.

2 Draw shapes on different coloured papers and cut them out. Glue the shapes on to the didgeridoo to decorate it.

34

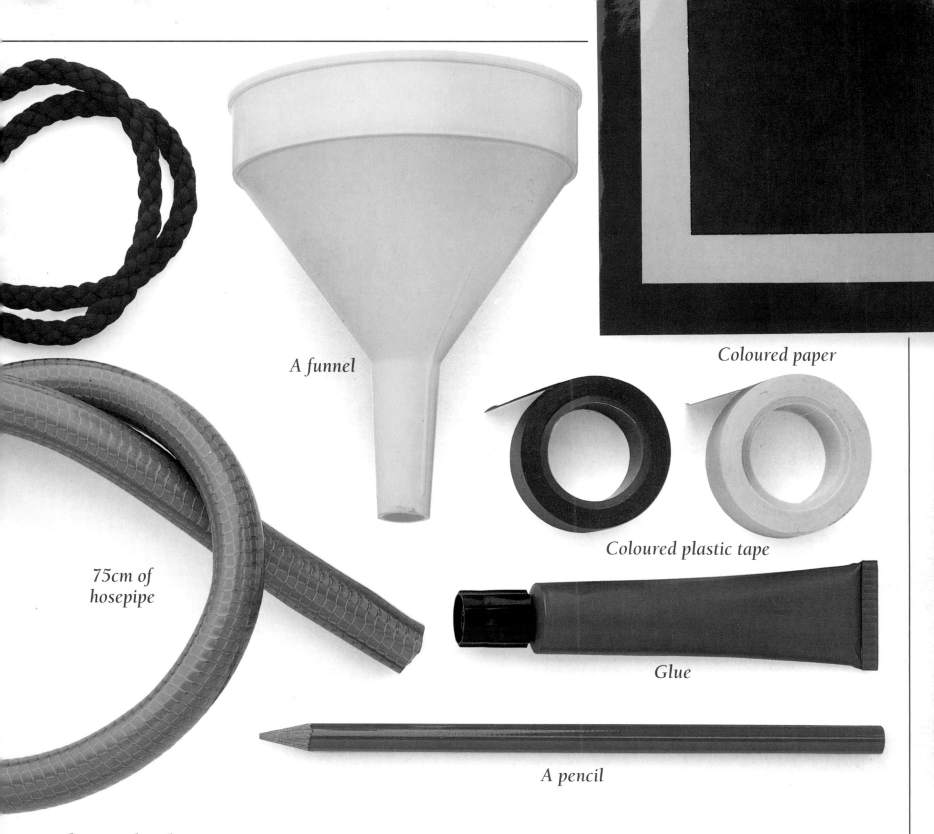

A funnel

Coloured paper

Coloured plastic tape

75cm of hosepipe

Glue

A pencil

Making the horn

1 Decorate the funnel with tape. Cut a 2 cm slit in one end of the hose. Push the funnel into the hose and tape it in place.

2 Make a large loop in the hose, and stick it in place with tape. Tape the pencil to the top of the loop, to give the horn shape.

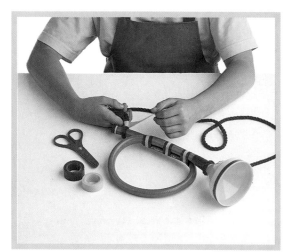

3 Decorate the horn with stripes of red and yellow tape. Tape the dressing-gown cord to both sides of the loop, as shown.

35

BLOW YOUR HORN

Here you can see the finished wind instruments. The didgeridoo is so long that we can only show part of it on this page! But if you look on page 46, you can see the whole didgeridoo being played in our orchestra.

You can find out how to play the didgeridoo and the horn in the playing steps below. They are both quite difficult to play at first, but with practice, you will soon be able to produce a good sound. Try making other notes with your horns by blowing harder or softer into the tubes and by tightening your lips as you blow.

Hosepipe Horn

LOUDSPEAKER
The funnel at the end of the horn acts like a loudspeaker and makes the horn sound louder.

Strip of red tape

Playing the horn

Hold the horn as shown. Blow a long, raspberry sound (making your lips vibrate) into the mouthpiece of the horn.

Playing the didgeridoo

Hold the didgeridoo over one half of your mouth, as shown. Purse your lips and blow a vibrating, raspberry sound into it.

Cardboard didgeridoo
You can decorate your didgeridoo with brightly coloured paper shapes, like the one shown here, or try painting it with poster paints, and then glazing it.

Red paper spot

Attach the dressing-gown cord to the horn with tape.

Strips of red and yellow insulating tape

The pencil holds the hosepipe straight, and stops the mouthpiece curling round.

Decorate the mouthpiece end of the horn with strips of red and yellow tape.

HORN STYLE!
Horn and bugle players often carry their instruments on brightly coloured cords or sashes, hanging diagonally across their chests.

Thin red paper strip

Long strip of blue paper cut into a wave pattern

MUSICAL BOXES

Musical instruments such as violins and guitars are simply specially-shaped wooden boxes with strings stretched across them. They produce a noise when their strings are plucked, strummed or played with a bow. Here you can see how to make your own stringed instruments from cardboard boxes and elastic bands. Turn the page to see the finished instruments, and to find out how to play them and change the note each string makes.

You will need

Thick, white card

A pencil

Coloured paper

3 small boxes and their lids

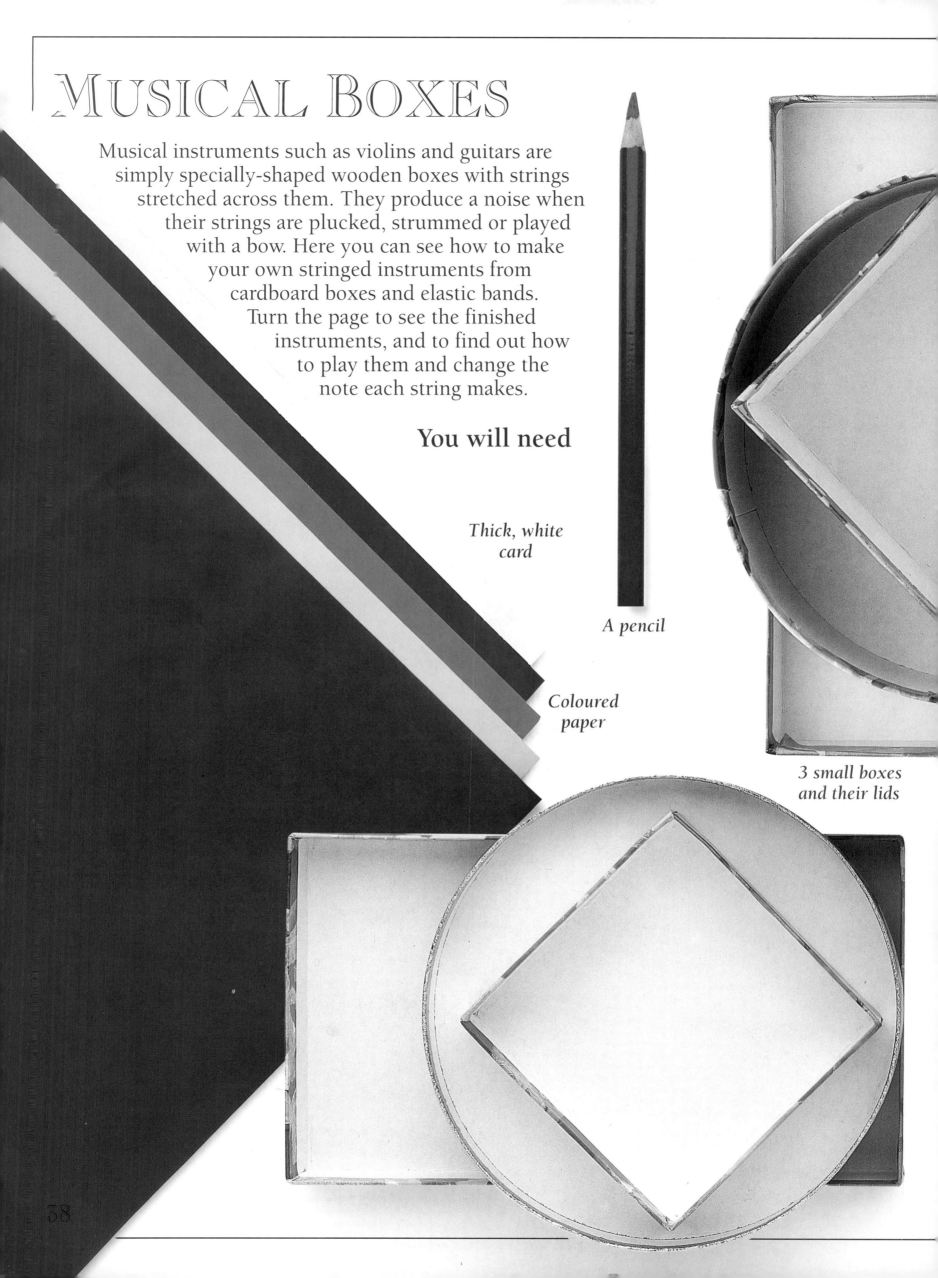

38

Glue

Yellow insulating tape

EQUIPMENT

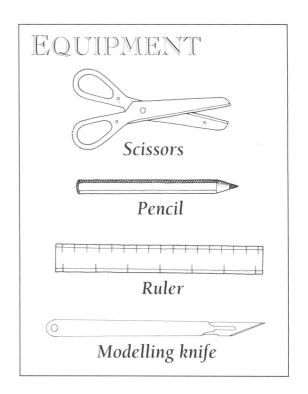

Scissors

Pencil

Ruler

Modelling knife

What to do

1 Cover the boxes and their lids with coloured paper. Line the bottom of each of the boxes with paper of a different colour.

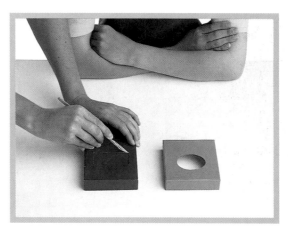

2 Choose a shape for the hole in the lid of the box, then draw it on the lid. Ask an adult to cut out the shape for you.

Making the bridge

Lots of elastic bands of different thicknesses, lengths and colours

3 Draw musical symbols and notes on coloured paper, then cut them out. Glue them around the sides of the box and on the lid.

4 Cut a strip of card as wide as your box and 5cm long. Cover the card in coloured paper. and fold it in half, lengthways.

STRING FEVER

Making the bridge

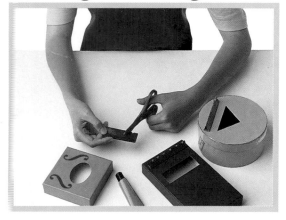

5 Cut notches along the card fold. Bend in the long edges of the card and glue them together to make a triangular prism.

Decorating the boxes

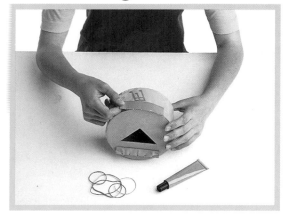

6 Glue the bridges in place. Make an extra flat bridge for the round box, and stick it to the side of the lid, as shown.

Finishing off

7 When the glue on the bridges is dry, stretch the elastic bands across the boxes. Slide a pencil under the bands on the box zither.

Here are the finished string boxes. The note each elastic band makes depends on three things: how thick the band is; how long the band is; and how tightly it is stretched across the box. You can find out how to play the instruments in the playing step opposite.

Red card bridge with six notches cut in it.

The longest strings make the lowest notes.

Box guitar

This circular box has two bridges, and five elastic bands of different thicknesses. The thickest bands make the lowest notes, and the thinnest make the highest notes.

Rectangular sounding-hole

Box zither

This rectangular box has six identical elastic bands stretched over it. You can change the notes the strings make by moving the pencil. When you move the pencil towards the bridge, you shorten the string. The shorter you make the string, the higher the note it will produce when you play it.

Red pencil

This flat bridge stops
the elastic bands
slipping off the box.

The inside of the
box is lined with
red paper.

Green card
bridge with
five notches

Triangular
sounding-hole

Decorate your box
with coloured
paper shapes.

The blue
elastic band
has been
stretched most,
so it makes the
highest note.

Blue card bridge
with four notches

Oval
sounding-hole

Playing the strings

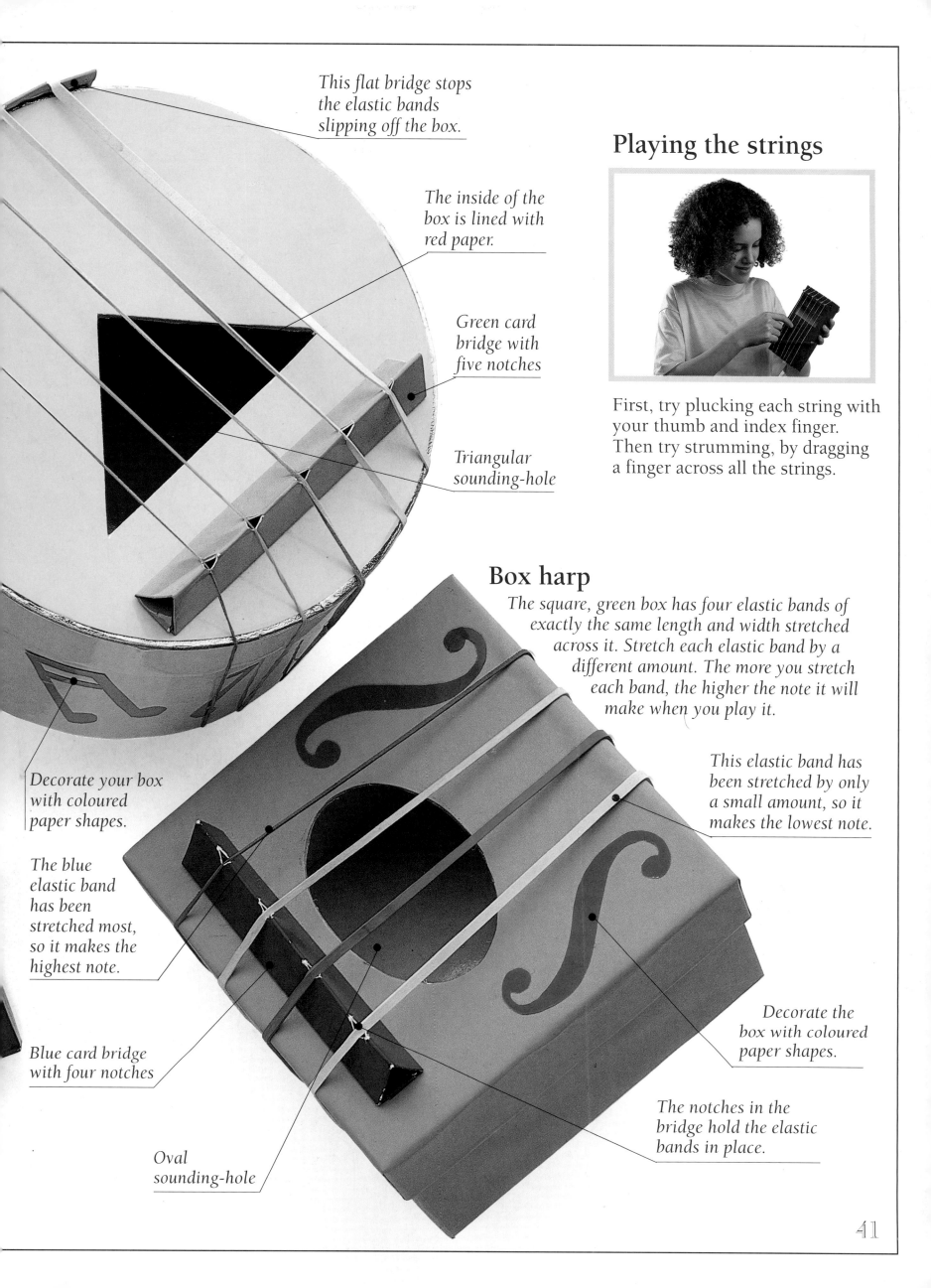

First, try plucking each string with
your thumb and index finger.
Then try strumming, by dragging
a finger across all the strings.

Box harp

*The square, green box has four elastic bands of
exactly the same length and width stretched
across it. Stretch each elastic band by a
different amount. The more you stretch
each band, the higher the note it will
make when you play it.*

This elastic band has
been stretched by only
a small amount, so it
makes the lowest note.

Decorate the
box with coloured
paper shapes.

The notches in the
bridge hold the elastic
bands in place.

41

MAKING A BANJO

This brilliant banjo has strings like the musical boxes, a skin like a drum, but you play it like a guitar. You will need to ask an adult to sand the piece of wood until it is smooth, and to help you cut the ice-cream tub. The rest is up to you. Turn the page to see the finished banjo and to find out how to tune and play your instrument.

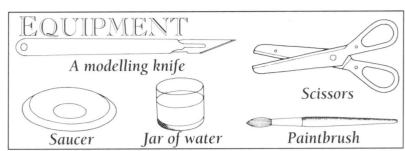
You will need

Blue insulating tape

Coloured poster paints

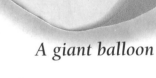

A giant balloon

Coloured ribbons

A piece of wood about 40cm long, 3.5cm wide and 1.5cm deep

3m fishing line

Some coloured paper

Stiff, white card

A round, plastic ice-cream tub

Four drawing pins

Eight eyelet screws

Varnish

PVA glue

What to do

1 Ask an adult to cut an 'I' shape 3.5cm long and 1.5cm wide, just under the rim of the tub. Cut another directly opposite it.

2 Bend out the flaps of the 'I', then thread the piece of wood through them, as shown. Pin the flaps securely to the wood.

3 Paint the banjo. Mix glue with the paint to help it stick to the tub. Let each colour dry before adding another. Varnish the banjo.

4 Cut the end off a balloon, and stretch the balloon over the tub. Tape it to the sides of the tub, then paint a design on the balloon.

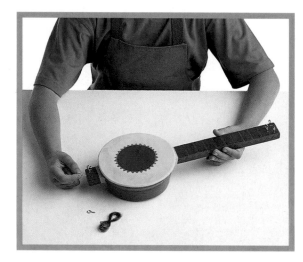

5 Screw four eyelets part-way into the wood at the top and bottom of the banjo. Make sure that you can twist each eyelet round.

6 Make two cardboard bridges, one 3.5cm long and the other 10cm long, as shown in steps 4 and 5 on pages 39 and 40.

43

BANJO MAGIC

Stringing the banjo

7 Tie a long piece of fishing line from each eyelet at the bottom of the banjo, to its opposite eyelet at the top. Snip off the excess line.

8 Put the two bridges under the banjo strings, as shown. Tighten the strings by turning the eyelets at the top of the banjo.

9 The banjo is now ready to tune. Decorate the banjo by tying coloured ribbons to the eyelets, as shown.

Ready to play

Here is the finished banjo. You can find out how to tune and play it on the opposite page.

The strings are stretched tight.

The balloon skin is stretched tightly over the ice-cream tub.

The design in the middle of the balloon matches the pattern along the neck of the banjo.

The long, card bridge is decorated with a thin strip of blue tape.

Notches cut into the bridge keep the strings in place.

The strings must be knotted securely to the eyelets.

Blue tape holds the balloon skin in place.

44

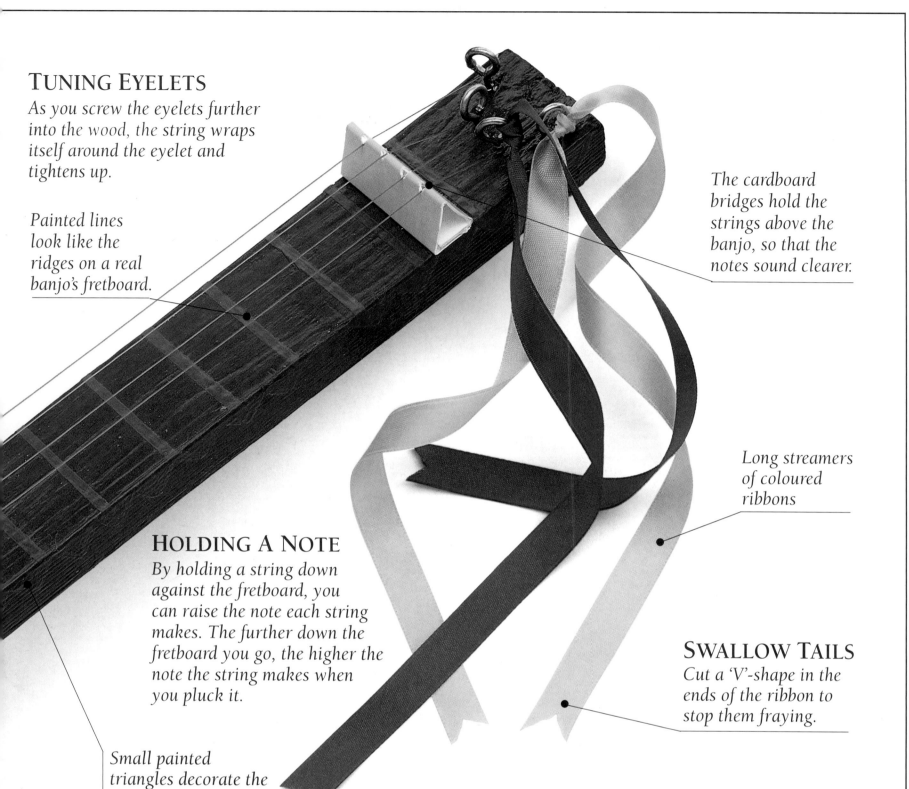

TUNING EYELETS

As you screw the eyelets further into the wood, the string wraps itself around the eyelet and tightens up.

Painted lines look like the ridges on a real banjo's fretboard.

The cardboard bridges hold the strings above the banjo, so that the notes sound clearer.

HOLDING A NOTE

By holding a string down against the fretboard, you can raise the note each string makes. The further down the fretboard you go, the higher the note the string makes when you pluck it.

Long streamers of coloured ribbons

SWALLOW TAILS

Cut a 'V'-shape in the ends of the ribbon to stop them fraying.

Small painted triangles decorate the neck of the banjo.

Strumming the banjo

Hold the strings down against the fretboard with one hand, rest your other hand on the tub, and brush your thumb across the strings.

Plucking the banjo

Hold the strings down against the fretboard, as before. Use the thumb and first finger of your other hand to pluck the strings, one at a time.

Tuning your banjo

Tune the banjo by tightening its strings. The tighter the string is, the higher the note it makes when you pluck it. To tighten a string, gradually screw the tuning eyelet further into the wood. As you do this, keep plucking the string until it makes the note you want. Tighten all the strings by slightly different amounts, so that each string makes a different note.

My First Orchestra

These children have formed an orchestra to play the instruments they have made. See if you can recognise the instruments they are playing. The musicians are grouped into four sections: **percussion** (instruments that you hit) in yellow T-shirts; **tuned percussion** (instruments that play a note when you hit them) in red T-shirts; **wind** (instruments that you blow into) in green T-shirts; and **strings** (instruments with tuned strings) in blue T-shirts. Try forming an orchestra or band with your friends.

MAKING MUSIC
On the next page, there is a piece of music for your orchestra to play.

YOUNG COMPOSER

Here you can find out how to make up your own rhythm music. First, choose an instrument to play and say its name over and over again. Next, hit or shake the instrument in time with this rhythm. Each name produces a different sound. Below, there are four rhythms for the orchestra to play together, in this way.

Once everyone can play the rhythms in time, experiment further by playing them quickly or slowly and loudly or softly. You could also try basing a rhythm on the names of the people in your orchestra, or on a favourite rhyme or song. Then see if you can write down your new rhythms in the way shown below.

Drum Hit the drum once slowly, as you say its name.	| | | | | | drum drum drum drum drum drum
Shakers Shake a shaker twice quickly, as you say its name.	|| || || || || || sha-ker sha-ker sha-ker sha-ker sha-ker sha-ker
Bubble organ Blow into or hit the bubble organ twice quickly, as you say each word of its name.	|| || || || || || bub-ble or-gan bub-ble or-gan bub-ble or-gan
Tambourines Shake the tambourine twice quickly and once slowly, as you say its name.	|| | || | || | tam-bour——ine tam-bour——ine tam-bour——ine
Pencil xylophone Hit one pencil twice quickly and another pencil once slowly, as you say the word 'xylophone'.	|| | || | || | xy-lo——phone xy-lo——phone xy-lo——phone
Triangle Hit the triangle once slowly and twice quickly, as you say its name.	| || | || | || tri——an-gle tri——an-gle tri——an-gle

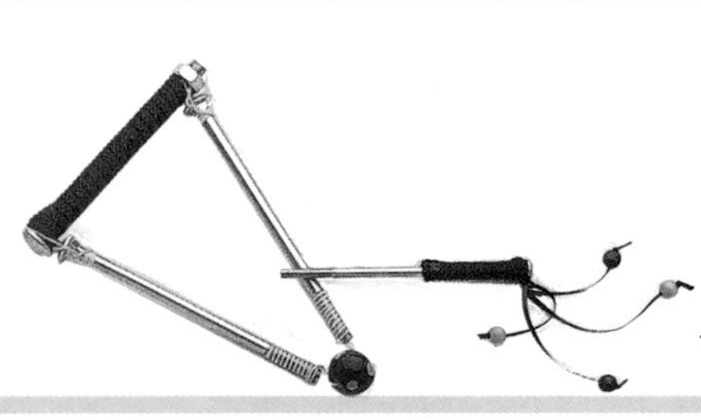